PHP
HTML
JAVASCRIPT
AJAX
JQUERY

PHP

PHP (P : PHP , HP: Hypertext Preprocessor)

❖ *FIND THE SMALLEST NUMBER USING PHP.*

PHP code for **finding and printing the smallest number** among four variables $a, $b, $c and $d :

```php
<?php

$a=5;
```

```
$b=7;

$c=1;

$d=8;

if($a<$b&&$a<$c&&$a<$d)

{

echo $a;

}

else if($b<$c&&$b<$d)

{

echo $b;
```

```php
}

else if($c<$d)

{

echo $c;

}

else

{

echo $d;

}

?>
```

RESULT :

1

EXPLANATION:

If $a is smaller than all others - print $a.

Else if $b is smaller than $c and $d - print $b.

Else if $c is smaller than $d - print $c.

Else - print $d.

BASICS OF PHP:

✧ **<?php** marks the beginning of PHP code.

✧ **?>** marks the end of PHP code. it's often omitted if the file contains only PHP code.

✧ In PHP, **$** is uscd to declare and access variables. For example:

$a =5; creates a variable $a and assigns it the value 5. $b, $c, and $d are also variables.

✧ **echo** is used to output (print) data to the screen. For example: echo $a; will print the value of $a (which is 5).

✧ **if, else if, and else**: These are conditional statements used to make decisions in the code. if checks a condition. If it's true, the code inside the if block runs.

✧ **else if** (or elseif) checks another condition.

✧ **$$** This is the logical *AND operator*. It checks if multiple conditions are true. For example "if $a is less than $b **and** $a is less than $c."

✧ { } These curly braces define a block of code. For example: The code inside { echo $a; } runs if

the if condition is true.

✧ The semicolon ; is used to end a

statement in PHP. For example: $a =

5; is a complete statement, so it ends

with a semicolon.

❖ *FIND GRADE USING PHP*

ACCORDING TO THE SCORES

ENTERED.

PHP code for printing a grade based on the score in $A by comparing it against certain threshold scores (90 - GRADE A, 80 - GRADE B, 70 - GRADE C.)

```php
<?php

$A=61;

$B=90;

$C=80;

$D=70;

IF($A>$B)
```

```
{

ECHO "GRADE A";

}

ELSE IF($A>$C)

{

ECHO "GRADE B";

}

ELSE IF($A>$D)

{

ECHO "GRADE C";
```

```
        }

ELSE

    {

ECHO "GRADE D";

    }

?>
```

RESULT:

GRADE D

EXPLANATION:

$A > $B? - 61 > 90 - No

$A > $C? - 61 > 80 - No

$A > $D? - 61 > 70 - No

Else - "GRADE D" is printed.

BASICS OF PHP

✧ **$_POST['A']** retrieves the value of the input field with name="A"

✧ **isset()** is a PHP function that checks if a variable is set and not null.

✧ **$_POST['S']** refers to the value of the input field with name="S" in the HTML form.

✧ **%**: Modulus operator (returns the remainder of a division).

✧ **==**: Equality operator (checks if two values are equal).

✧ **<input>**: HTML tag for creating input fields.

✧ **type="text"**: Specifies a text input field.

- ✧ **type="submit"**: Specifies a submit button.

- ✧ **name**: Assigns a name to an input field (used in PHP to retrieve its value).

- ✧ **value**: Sets the default value of the text on a submit button.

❖ *FIND GRADE USING PHP POST METHOD*

This PHP code will create a simple web form that takes a name and marks from the user, then it will print the name and shows the grade of the student based on the marks entered.

```php
<?PHP

IF(ISSET($_POST['S']))

{

$A =$_POST['A'];

ECHO $A;

$B=$_POST['B'];
```

```
IF($B>=90)

{

ECHO "GRADE A";

}

ELSE IF($B>80)

{

ECHO "GRADE B";

}

ELSE IF($B>70)

{
```

```php
ECHO "GRADE C";

}

ELSE

{

ECHO "GRADE D";

}

}

?>

<HTML>

<HEAD>
```

```
</HEAD>

<BODY>

<FORM METHOD="POST">

NAME<INPUT TYPE="TEXT"

NAME="A">

MARK <INPUT TYPE="TEXT"

NAME="B">

<INPUT TYPE="SUBMIT" NAME="S"

VALUE="SUBMIT">

</FORM>
```

</BODY>

</HTML>

 Example if the user type:

Name: ELIZABETH

Mark: 85

RESULT :

ELIZABETH GRADE B.

EXPLANATION :

Creates a form for the user to type:

Name - stored in $_POST['A']

Marks - stored in $_POST['B']

When "SUBMIT" is clicked, the data is sent to the same page using the POST method.

isset($_POST['S']) - checks if the form was submitted.

Displays the entered name (echo $A;).

Checks the marks ($B) and decides:

If mark is 90 or more - Grade A

If mark is 81–89 - Grade B

If mark is 71–80 - Grade C

If mark is 70 or less - Grade D

❖ *FIND ODD OR EVEN NUMBER*

USING PHP

Php code for creatinga a web form, where user can enter a number and as submit button is pressed,it will check whether the number user entered is odd or even.

```php
<?php

if(isset($_POST['S']))

{

$W=$_POST['A'];
```

```php
IF($W%2==1)

{

ECHO "$W IS ODD";

}

else {

ECHO "$W IS EVEN";

}

}

?>

<HTML>
```

```html
<HEAD>

</HEAD>

<BODY>

<FORM METHOD="POST">

<input type="text" name="A">


<input type="SUBMIT" name="S"

VALUE="SUBMIT">

</FORM>
```

```
</BODY>

</HTML>
```

RESULT:

User types: 9 - 9 IS ODD

User types: 8→ 8 IS EVEN

EXPLANATION:

isset($_POST['S']) - checks if the submit button was pressed.

$W = $_POST['A']; - stores the entered number in $W.

if ($W % 2 == 1) - checks the remainder when dividing by 2:

If remainder is 1, the number is odd - print "W IS ODD".

Else, the number is even - print "W IS EVEN".

❖ *FOR LOOP ASCENDING ORDER*

USING POST METHOD

PHP code is for printing all numbers in a range entered by the user.

```php
<?php

IF(ISSET($_POST['S']))

{

$A=$_POST['X'];
```

```php
$B=$_POST['Y'];

for($i=$A;$i<=$B;$i++)

{

echo "$i<br>";

}

}

?>

<html>

<head></head>
```

```
<body>

<form method="POST">

<input type="text" name="X">

<input type="text" name="Y">

<input type="SUBMIT" name="S"

VALUE="OK">

</form>

</body>

</html>
```

RESULT:

If you enter x-5 and y-9 output will be:

5

6

7

8

9

EXPLANATION:

When the form is submitted, it checks if the submit button is set.

$A gets the value from X.

$B gets the value from Y.

A for loop starts from $A and runs until $B, printing each number on a new line (<br>).

❖ *FOR LOOP DESCENDING ORDER USING POST METHOD.*

PHP code is for printing numbers in descending order from two numbers entered by the user.

```php
<?php

if(isset($_POST['S']))

{

$A=$_POST['N'];

$B=$_POST['M'];

for($i=$A;$i>=$B;$i--)

{

echo "$i<br/>";

}
```

```
}

?>

<html>

<head></head>

<body>

<form method="POST">

<INPUT TYPE="TEXT" NAME="N">


<INPUT TYPE="TEXT" NAME="M">
```

```
<INPUT TYPE="SUBMIT" NAME="S"

VALUE="OK">
```

```
</form>
```

```
</body>
```

```
</html>
```

RESULT:

If you enter n-15 m-10

Output will be :

15

14

13

12

11

10

EXPLANATION:

Checks if the form was submitted.

Stores the values of N and M in $A and $B.

Uses a for loop starting from $A to $B.

Prints each number with a
 (line break).

❖ FOR LOOP ACSENDING ORDER

PHP code for printing numbers from 1 to 10 in ascending order on the same line.

```php
<?php

for($i=1;$i<=10;$i++)

{

echo $i;

}
```

?>

RESULT:

12345678910

EXPLANATION:

for($i=1; $i<=10; $i++) - starts from 1

and increases by 1 until it reaches 10.

echo $i; - displays each number.

❖ FOR LOOP DESCENDING ORDER

PHP code for printing numbers from 10 down to 1 in descending order, each on a new line.

```php
<?php

for($i=10;$i>=1;$i--)

{

echo "$i<br/>";
```

```
    }

    ?>
```

RESULT :

1

2

3

4

5

6

7

8

9

10

EXPLANATION:

for($i=10; $i>=1; $i--) - prints numbers from 10 and decrements by 1 until it reaches 1.

echo "$i
"; - displays the current number and moves to a new line (<br/>).

❖ *PRINT ODD NUMBER ONLY USING POST METHOD*

This PHP code for displaying all odd numbers between two numbers entered by the user.

```php
<?php

if(isset($_POST['S']))

{
```

```php
$A=$_POST['A'];

$B=$_POST['B'];



$i=$A;

while($i<=$B)

{

if($i%2==1)

{

echo "$i<br/>";

}
```

```php
        $i++;

    }

}

?>
```

```html
<html>

<head>

</head>

<body>

<form method="POST">

<input type="text" name="A">
```

```
<input type="text" name="B">

<input type="SUBMIT" name="S"

VALUE="SUBMIT">

</form>

</body>

</html>
```

RESULT:

If user enter:

A = 5

B = 10

It will display output

5

7

9

EXPLANATION:

A submit button (SUBMIT) sends the data using POST.

 Checks if the form is submitted.

Starts from $A and loops while $i <= $B using a while loop.

Inside the loop, if($i % 2 == 1) checks if the number is odd.

If odd, it prints it with a
 (new line).

Increments $i by 1 in each loop.

- ***WHILE LOOP ASCENDING ORDER***

PHP code for printing numbers from 1 to 10 in ascending order using a while loop.

```php
<?php

$i=1;
```

```php
while($i<=10)

{

echo "$i<br/>";

$i++;

}

?>
```

RESULT :

1

2

3

4

5

6

7

8

9

10

EXPLANATION:

$i = 1; - starting value.

while($i <= 10) - keeps looping until $i becomes greater than 10.

echo "$i
"; - prints the current number and moves to a new line.

$i++; - increases $i by 1 each time.

- ***WHILE LOOP ASCENDING ORDER USING POST METHOD***

PHP code for printing all numbers in ascending order from a starting number to an ending number entered by the user.

```php
<?php

if(isset($_POST['S']))

{

$X=$_POST['A'];

$Y=$_POST['B'];


$i=$X;

while($i<=$Y)

{

echo "$i<br/>";
```

```php
        $i++;

    }

}

?>
```

<html><head></head>

<body>

<form method="POST">

<input type="text" name="A">

<input type="text" name="B">
```
```

```
<input type="SUBMIT" name="S"

VALUE="SUBMIT">

</form>

</body></html>
```

RESULT:

If user enter:

A = 3

B = 9

It will print

3

4

5

6

7

8

9

EXPLANATION:

A submit button sends the values via POST.

Checks if the form is submitted.

Sets $i to the starting number $X.

Uses a while loop: keeps printing $i and incrementing it until it reaches $Y.

❖ *BACKGROUND COLOR USING POST METHOD*

PHP code for changing the web page background color based on the option the user selects from a dropdown list.

```php
<?php

IF(ISSET($_POST['S']))

{

$A=$_POST['A'];

IF($A=='P')

{

?>

<BODY BGCOLOR="RED"></BODY>

<?PHP

}
```

```php
IF($A=='Q')

{

?>

<BODY BGCOLOR="pink"></BODY>

<?PHP

}

IF($A=='R')

{

?>
```

```
<BODY

BGCOLOR="GREEN"></BODY>

<?PHP

}

}

?>

<IITML>

<HEAD>

</HEAD>

<BODY>
```

```
<FORM METHOD="POST">

<SELECT NAME="A">

<OPTION

VALUE="P">RED</OPTION>

<OPTION

VALUE="Q">pink</OPTION>

<OPTION

VALUE="R">GREEN</OPTION>

</SELECT>
```

```
<INPUT TYPE="SUBMIT" NAME="S"

VALUE="SUBMIT">

</FORM>

</BODY>

</HTML>
```

RESULT: If user choose Pink and submit - the page reloads with a pink background.

EXPLANATION:

A dropdown (<select>) has three options:

P - Red

Q - Pink

R - Green

When you select a color and click Submit, the form sends the value via POST.

 Checks if the form is submitted (isset($_POST['S'])).

Reads the selected value from $_POST['A'].

If:

Value is P - set <body bgcolor="RED">. Changes web page background color to Red.

Value is Q - set <body bgcolor="pink">. Changes web page background color to Pink.

Value is R - set <body bgcolor="GREEN">. Changes web page background color to Green.

❖ CONVERT TEXT INTO REVERSE, UPPERCASE, LOWERCASE AND FIND ITS LENGTH

PHP code for performing different text operations on a string entered by the user, depending on which button is clicked.

```php
<?php

IF(ISSET($_POST['SUB']))

{
```

```php
$A=$_POST['A'];

ECHO STRLEN($A);

}

IF(ISSET($_POST['SUB1']))

{

$A=$_POST['A'];

ECHO STRREV($A);

}

IF(ISSET($_POST['SUB2']))

{
```

```php
$A=$_POST['A'];

ECHO STRTOUPPER($A);

}

IF(ISSET($_POST['SUB3']))

{

$A=$_POST['A'];

ECHO STRTOLOWER($A);

}


?>
```

```
<HTML>

<HEAD>


</HEAD>

<BODY>

<FORM METHOD="POST">

<INPUT TYPE="TEXT" NAME–"A">

<INPUT TYPE="SUBMIT"

NAME="SUB" VALUE="LENGTH">
```

```
<INPUT TYPE="SUBMIT"
NAME="SUB1" VALUE="REVERSE">


<INPUT TYPE="SUBMIT"
NAME="SUB2" VALUE="UPPER">


<INPUT TYPE="SUBMIT"
NAME="SUB3" VALUE="LOWER">


</FORM>
```

</BODY>

</HTML>

RESULT:

If user types HELLO

LENGTH - 5

REVERSE - olleH

UPPER - HELLO

LOWER - hello

EXPLANATION:

A text box where the user types any word or sentence.

Four submit buttons will be there:

LENGTH - show number of characters in the text.

REVERSE - display the text backwards.

UPPER - convert text to uppercase.

LOWER - convert text to lowercase.

If LENGTH is clicked - strlen($A) gives the number of characters.

If REVERSE is clicked - strrev($A) reverses the text.

If UPPER is clicked - strtoupper($A) converts it to all uppercase letters.

If LOWER is clicked - strtolower($A) converts it to all lowercase letters.

❖ *CREATE A MULTIPLICATION TABLE USING PHP*

PHP code to print multiplication results between two limits.

```php
<?php

if (isset($_POST['S'])) {

$A = $_POST['A'];

$B = $_POST['B'];

    $C = $_POST['C'];

$i = $A;

while ($i <= $B) {

$R = $i * $C;
```

```php
echo "$i * $C = $R<br/>";

$i++;

}

}

?>
```

```html
<html>

<hcad>

<title>Multiplication Table</title>

</head>

<body>
```

```html
<form method="POST">

FIRST LIMIT: <input type="text"
name="A"><br/>

SECOND LIMIT: <input type="text"
name="B"><br/>

MULTIPLY BY: <input type="text"
name="C"><br/>

<input type="submit" name="S"
value="MULTIPLY">

</form>
```

```
</body>

</html>
```

RESULT:

A = 2

B = 5

C = 3

2 * 3 = 6

3 * 3 = 9

4 * 3 = 12

5 * 3 = 15

❖ *FIND MAXIMUM OR MINIMUM AMONG TWO NUMBERS*

❖ PHP code for finding **the smaller** and **the larger** number between two given inputs, depending on which button you click.

```php
<?php

IF(ISSET($_POST['Z']))
```

```php
{

$A=$_POST['A'];

$B=$_POST['B'];



$F=MIN($A,$B);

ECHO "MIN$F";

}



IF(ISSET($_POST['S']))
```

```php
{

$C=$_POST['C'];

$D=$_POST['D'];

$E=MAX($C,$D);

ECHO "MAX$E";

}

?>
```

<html>

<head></head>

<body>

```
<form method="POST">

<INPUT TYPE="TEXT" NAME="A">

<INPUT TYPE="TEXT" NAME="B">


<INPUT TYPE="SUBMIT" NAME="Z"

VALUE="MIN">


<INPUT TYPE="TEXT"  NAME="C">

<INPUT TYPE="TEXT" NAME="D">
```

```
<INPUT TYPE="SUBMIT" NAME="S"

VALUE="MAX">

</form>

</body>

</html>
```

RESULT:

If user enter:

A = 5, B = 8 - Click MIN - Output:

MIN5

C = 4, D = 2 - Click MAX - Output:

MAX4

EXPLANATION:

MIN button

Takes values from input fields A and B.

Uses PHP's MIN() function to find the smaller of the two.

Prints the result as MIN<value> when user click the MIN button.

MAX button

Takes values from input fields C and D.

Uses PHP's MAX() function to find the larger of the two.

Prints the result as MAX<value> when user click the MAX button.

❖ **PRINT NUMBER OF TEXT, TEXT AREA, PASSWORD AND FILE COLUMN ACCORDING TO THE GIVEN NUMBER**

PHP code for generating form input fields based on the user's choice and the number they enter.

```php
<?php

IF(ISSET($_POST['Z']))

{

$E=$_POST['A'];

$F=$_POST['B'];


IF($F=='P')
```

```php
{

FOR($i=1;$i<=$E;$i++)

{

?>

<input type="text">

<?php

}

}

if($F=='Q')

{
```

```php
FOR($i=1;$i<=$E;$i++)

{

?>

<textarea></textarea>

<?php

}

}

if($F=='R')

{

FOR($i=1;$i<=$E;$i++)
```

```php
    {

    ?>

    <input type="file">

    <?php

    }

    }

    if($F=='S')

    {

    FOR($i=1;$i<=$E;$i++)

    {
```

```php
?>

<input type="password">

<?php

}

}

}

?>

<html>

<head>
```

```html
</head>

<body>

<form method="POST">

ENTER LIMIT <INPUT TYPE="TEXT"

NAME="A">

<SELECT NAME="B">

<OPTION

VALUE="P">TEXT</OPTION>

<OPTION

VALUE="Q">TEXTAREA</OPTION>
```

```
<OPTION
VALUE="R">FILE</OPTION>
<OPTION
VALUE="S">PASSWORD</OPTION>
</SELECT>
<INPUT TYPE="SUBMIT" NAME="Z"
VALUE="SUBMIT">
</form>
</body>
</html>
```

RESULT:

A = 4

B = TEXT

<input type="text">

<input type="text">

<input type="text">

<input type="text">

EXPLANATION:

User enters a number (how many inputs to create)

User selects a type of form element from the drop down

P - creates that many <input type="text"> boxes.

Q - creates that many <textarea> boxes.

R - creates that many <input type="file"> file upload fields.

S - creates that many <input type="password"> fields.

When you click SUBMIT, PHP loops from 1 to the limit you entered and prints that type of field multiple times.

❖ FINDING THE MAXIMUM OR MINIMUM VALUE

PHP code for finding the maximum or minimum value from a list of numbers that the user enters.

<HTML>

```
<HEAD></HEAD>

<BODY>

<FORM METHOD="POST">

<INPUT TYPE="TEXT" NAME="A">

<INPUT TYPE="SUBMIT" NAME="S"

VALUE="SUBMIT">

<?PHP

IF(ISSET($_POST['S']))

{

$A=$_POST['A'];
```

```php
FOR($i=1;$i<=$A;$i++)

{

?>

<INPUT TYPE="TEXT" NAME="M[]">

<?PHP

}

?>

<INPUT TYPE="SUBMIT" NAME="Z"
VALUE="MAX">
```

```php
<INPUT TYPE="SUBMIT" NAME="Y"

VALUE="MIN">

<?PHP

}

IF(ISSET($_POST['Z']))

{

$w=$_POST['M'];

ECHO MAX($w);

}

IF(ISSET($_POST['Y']))
```

```php
{

$V=$_POST['M'];

ECHO MIN($V);

}


?>
```

</FORM>

</BODY>

</HTML>

RESULT:

For example-

If user Enter 4 - click SUBMIT - 4 input boxes appear.

 Enter 12, 26, 4, 19

Click MAX - Output: 26

Click MIN - Output: 4

EXPLANATION:

User enters a number in A

According to this number input boxes will be shown for entering values.

Example: If user enter 3 and click SUBMIT, it will generate 3 text boxes.

User fills those boxes. The boxes are named M[] (an array), so all values will be stored together in an array.

User clicks MAX or MIN

If MAX is clicked - It uses MAX($w) to find the largest number.

If MIN is clicked - It should use MIN($V) to find the smallest number,

- ***CREATE A CALCULATOR USING PHP [SWITCH METHOD]***

 PHP code for a simple calculator built with HTML and Bootstrap styling.

<?PHP

```php
IF(ISSET($_POST['SUB']))

{

$A=$_POST['A'];

$B=$_POST['B'];

$W=$_POST['R'];

switch ($W)

{

case "+" : $R=$A+$B;

echo $R;

break;
```

```
case "-" : $R=$A-$B;

echo $R;

break;

case "/"  : $R=$A/$B;

echo $R;

break;

case "*"  : $R=$A*$B;

echo $R;

break;

}
```

```
    }

?>

<HTML>

<HEAD>

<link href="bootstrap-3.4.1-

dist/bootstrap-3.4.1-

dist/css/bootstrap.min.css"

rel="stylesheet" type="text/css"/>


</HEAD>
```

```html
<BODY>

<FORM METHOD="POST">


<table class="table table-responsive"
style="background-color: red;color:
black;font-family: fantasy">

<tr><td>

NO<INPUT TYPE="TEXT"
NAME="A"></td>
```

```html
<td> <SELECT NAME="R"
class="form-control">
<OPTION>-</OPTION>
<OPTION>+</OPTION>
<OPTION>/</OPTION>
<OPTION>*</OPTION>
</SELECT></td>
<td>NO<INPUT TYPE="TEXT"
NAME="B"></td></tr>
```

```
<tr><td> <INPUT TYPE="SUBMIT"

NAME="SUB"

VALUE="SUBMIT"></td></tr></table>

</FORM>

</BODY>

</HTML>
```

RESULT:

If user enter

A = 18

B = 9

And selects Operator = / from dropdown list

Output will be 2

EXPLANATION:

When user enter First number (A) and

Second number (B) and

An operation from the dropdown (R) - +, -, /,

When the user click SUBMIT

PHP checks which operator you selected using a switch statement.

Performs the corresponding calculation:

And Displays the result.

HTML

BASICS ABOUT HTML

Hypertext markup language. It is a scripting language used to create static websites.

It contains predefined keywords called tags. Tags are mainly two types empty tags and container tags.

Container tags eg : <abc>

Empty tags eg:

There are some basic tags which are used everywhere in HTML.

They are:

<HTML>

<HEAD>

<TITLE>

</TITLE >

</HEAD>

<BODY>

</BODY>

</HTML>

It mainly contains a head and body.Title tags will always come inside head tags.

It will start and end with HTML tags <HTML> </HTML>

You can use notepad to do HTML coding.

Always save the file as   Filename.html

And remember to Save as all files.

Tags

Heading tags are:

<h1> </h1>

<h2> </h2>

<h3> </h3>

<h4> </h4>

<h5> </h5>

\<h6\>   \</h6\>

Let's see   use heading tags:

```
<h1>my first page </h1>
<h2>my first page </h2>
<h3>my first page </h3>
<h4>my first page </h4>
<h5>my first page </h5>
<h6>my first page </h6>
```

---

my first page

my first page

my first page

my first page

my first page

my first page

Some important tags:

 :Break tag used to break a sentence .

<p> </p> v paragraph tag used to write paragraph

<b> </b> : bold tag used to write bold letters

<i> </i> : italics used to write italic letters

<u> </u> : used to underline a sentence

\<sub\> \</sub\> : sub script

eg: H \<sub\>2 \</sub\> SO \<sub\>4 \</sub\>

\<sup\>\</sup\> : super script

The HTML codes for creating a page as

below is

```
<HTML>
<head>
<title>first page of html</title>
</head>
<body bgcolor="red">
<h1>
<font color="white" face="fantasy">
My first page </font>
</h1>
</body>
<html>
```

Notice the background color of the page is red. bgcolor="red" which we wrote inside the body tag

<body bgcolor="red">

We wrote My first page inside H1 tag

<h1>My first page </h1>

font color is white and font face is fantasy

<h1><font color="white" face="fantasy">My first page</font> </h1>

We wrote everything inside the basic html head body tags

Tables

create a table

Table tags includes:

Tr : table row

Td : table data

Th : table heading

For eg:

Country	capital
India	New delhi
Germany	Berlin
New zealand	Wellington

HTML Coding for the above table is

<html>

<head>

<style>

```
table, th, td {

border: 1px solid black;

}



</style>

</head>



<body>



<table style="width:50%">
```

```
<tr>

<th>Country</th>

<th>capital</th>



</tr>



<tr>

<td>India</td>

<td>New delhi</td>

</tr>
```

```
<tr>

<td>Germany</td>

<td>Berlin</td>


</tr>



<tr>

<td>New zealand</td>

<td>Wellington</td>
```

```
</tr>

</table>



</body>

</html>
```

Here we use the style tags inside the head tags to define width of table border which is 1px and border color which is solid black.

Width of the table 50 % is given by using style inside the table tag

<table style="width:50%">

Then we create the four rows using tr tags

Form controls

Coding for the above form is :

<html>

<head>

</head>

<body>

Text field : <input type="text" name ="n"

Password : <input

type="Password" name="p" />

Dropdown list : <select name="country">

<option> India</option>

<option>Brazil </option>

```
<option>America </option>

<option> England </option>

</select><br/>



Radio button : <input

type="radio" name="rd" value="m" />

male<br/>
```

```
<input type="radio" name="rd" value="f"

/> female<br/>
```

Checkbox:

```
<input

type="checkbox" name="chk"/>English
```

```
<input

type="checkbox" name="chk"/>Chineese
```

```html
<input

type="checkbox" name="chk"/>Japanese

<br/>


Submit button: <input

type="submit" name="sub"

value="register"/>


</body>
```

</html>

Here we have created a :

textfield

Password field

Dropdown list

Radio button

Check box and a

Submit button

We have used input type , name and some places value attributes.

Lists

Listing are mainly two types ordered and unordered

Unordered list: ul

Ordered list: ol

List :li

Unordered List

- India
- America
- England
- China

Coding for the above unordered list is :

<html>

<head>

Unordered List

</head>

<body>

<ul>

<li>India </li>

<li>America </li>

<li>England </li>

<li>China</li>

```
</ul>
```

```
</body>
```

```
</html>
```

Ordered list:

Ordered List

1. India
2. America
3. England
4. China

Coding for the above ordered list is:

```html
<html>

<head>

Ordered List

</head>


<body>

<ol>

<li>India </li>

<li>America </li>
```

```html
<li>England </li>

<li>China </li>

</ol>

</body>

</html>
```

❖ PHP PALLINDROME.

PHP code to test if a word is a palindrome (eg: madam) and perform rounding operations on a number.

```php
<?php
```

```php
if (isset($_POST['S'])) {

$W = $_POST['X'];

input box

$E = strrev($W);

if ($W == $E) {

echo "<p>$W is a PALINDROME</p>";

} else {

echo "<p>$W is NOT a

PALINDROME</p>";

}
```

```php
}


if (isset($_POST['R'])) {

$A = $_POST['O'];

input

echo "<p>Rounded value of $A is: " .

round($A) . "</p>";

}

if (isset($_POST['C'])) {

$B = $_POST['O'];
```

```php
echo "<p>Ceil value of $B is: " . ceil($B) .

"</p>";

}




if (isset($_POST['F'])) {

$C = $_POST['O'];

echo "<p>Floor value of $C is: " .

floor($C) . "</p>";

}

?>
```

```html
<html>

<head>

<title>Palindrome & Number

Rounding</title>

</head>

<body>

<form method="POST">

<!-- Palindrome check -->

<label>Enter a word:</label>

<input type="text" name="X">
```

```html
<input type="submit" name="S"

value="PALINDROME">

<br><br>

<!-- Number rounding -->

<label>Enter a number:</label>

<input type="text" name="O">

<input type="submit" name="R"

value="ROUND">

<input type="submit" name="C"

value="CEIL">
```

```html
<input type="submit" name="F"

value="FLOOR">

</form>

</body>

</html>
```

❖ *ARRAYS*

● **FOREACH ARRAY**

Printing all values from an array

(numbers and strings) one per line.

```php
<?php
```

```php
$A=ARRAY(6,8,9,7,6,'KKK',9,'OOO');

FOREACH($A AS $B)

{

ECHO "$B<BR/>";

}

?>
```

RESULT :

6

8

9

7

6

KKK

9

OOO

● *FUNCTION WITH ARGUMENTS*

PHP function that calculates the sum of three numbers and prints the result.

```php
<?php

FUNCTION SUM($A,$B,$C)

{

$D=$A+$B+$C;

ECHO $D;

}

SUM(6,99,8 )

?>
```

Here $D stores the sum of $A + $B + $C.

RESULT : 113

● *FUNCTION WITH RETURN TYPE*

PHP function that subtracts two numbers and returns the result.

```php
<?php

FUNCTION SUBTRACT($A,$B)

{

$C=$A-$B;

RETURN $C;

}
```

```
$D=SUBTRACT(6,8);

ECHO $D;

?>
```

RESULT:

```
$D = SUBTRACT(16, 8);

ECHO $D;
```

PRINTS 8

EXPLANATION:

Takes two parameters: $A and $B

Subtracts $B from $A

Returns the result

● *MATH FUNCTION*

This PHP code is for finding powers, square roots, maximum/minimum values, and rounding numbers.

```php
<?php

$a=pow(4,6);

echo "$a<br/>";

$b=sqrt(79);
```

```php
echo "$b<br/>";

$c=max(56,87);

echo "$c<br/>";

$d=min(5,8);

echo "$d<br/>";

$e=round(5.7);

echo "$e<br/>";

$f=ceil(6.8);

echo "$f<br/>";

$g=floor(3.7);
```

```php
echo "$g<br/>";

?>
```

RESULT :

4096

8.8881944173156

87

5

6

7

3

EXPLANATION :

pow(x, y) - Raises a number to a power.

sqrt(x) - Finds the square root.

max(x, y) - Returns the larger value.

min(x, y) - Returns the smaller value.

round(x) - Rounds the given number to the nearest integer.

ceil(x) - Always rounds up the number.

floor(x) - Always rounds down the number.

- ***PHP FRONTEND***

PHP code to display each key and value from an associative array in a key-value format.

```php
<?php

$a=array("php"=>"frontend","mysql"=>"backend");
```

```php
foreach($a as $k=>$v)

{

echo "$k-$v<br/>";

}

?>
```

RESULT :

php-frontend

mysql-backend

EXPLANATION :

$a is an **associative array**

foreach ($a as $k => $v) means:

    $k - key (e.g., "php")

    $v - value (e.g., "frontend")

echo "$k-$v
"; prints them in key-value format, one per line.

● *PHP ARRAY*

```php
<?PHP

$A=ARRAY(2,3,4,1,2,3,'NAJI');

ECHO $A[6];

?>
```

RESULT : NAJI

This code is for printing the value at a specific position (index 6) in an array.

❖ *PUSH OR POP ARRAY*

PHP code to add, remove, and sort elements in ascending order and in descending order in an array in PHP.

```php
<?php

$W=ARRAY(4,5,6,3,9);

ARRAY_PUSH($W,10,10);

FOREACH($W AS $B)

{

ECHO "$B";
```

```php
}

array_pop($W);

ECHO"<BR/>";

foreach($W AS $B)

{

ECHO"$B";

}

SORT($W);

ECHO"<BR/>";

FOREACH($W AS $B)
```

```
{

ECHO "$B";

}

RSORT($W);

ECHO"<BR/>";

FOREACH($W AS $B)

{

ECHO"$B";

}

?>
```

RESULT :

456391010   ← after push

4563910   ← after pop

13456910   ← after sort

10965431   ← after rsort

EXPLANATION :

array_push() - adds one or more elements

to the end of an array.

array_pop() - removes the last element

from an array.

sort() - sorts the array in ascending order.

rsort() - sorts the array in descending order.

foreach - loops through the array to display values.

❖ ARRAY INSIDE AN ARRAY

PHP code for accessing and printing every value from a multidimensional array using nested loops.

```php
<?php
```

```php
$a=array(array(1,3,2),array(6,'ll','tree'),array(5,7,'ELIZABETH'));

foreach($a as $b)

{

foreach($b as $c)

{

echo "$c<br/>";

}

}

?>
```

RESULT :

1

3

2

6

ll

tree

5

7

ELIZABETH

EXPLANATION :

$a is a **multidimensional array** — an array containing other arrays.

The **outer** foreach ($b) loops through each sub-array.

The **inner** foreach ($c) loops through each value inside the current sub-array.

echo "$c
"; prints each element on its own line.

❖ ECHO ALL ARRAYS

PHP code for accessing array elements by index and printing them one by one using a for loop.

```php
<?php

$A=array(6,5,5,4,6,'jasmine','lilly');

for($i=0;$i<=6;$i++)

echo "$A[$i]<br/>";

?>
```

RESULT :

6

5

5

4

6

jasmine

lilly

EXPLANATION :

- $A is contains numbers and strings.

- The for loop starts with $i = 0 and runs while $i <= 6.

- Each loop iteration prints the element at index $i.

-
 moves to a new line after each output.

❖ SIMPLE FUNCTIONS

PHP code for adding two predefined numbers inside a function and printing the sum when the function is called.

```php
<?php

FUNCTION SUM()

{

$A=7;

$B=6;

$C=$A+$B;

ECHO $C;
```

```
}

SUM();

?>
```

RESULT : 13

EXPLANATION :

$A is set to 7

$B is set to 6

$C stores their sum (13)

echo prints the result.

JAVASCRIPT

❖ PRINT NATURAL NUMBERS

```
<html>

<head>

<script>

function ee()

{

var

a=document.getElementById("j").value;
```

```javascript
var
b=document.getElementById("k").value;


for(var i=a;i<=b;i++)

{

document.getElementById("p").innerHT

ML+=i+"<br>";

}

}

</script>
```

```html
</head>

<body>

<input type="text" id="j">

<input type="text" id="k">

<input type="button" value="Natural No"

onclick="ee()">

<p id="p"></p>

</body>

</html>
```

This HTML , JavaScript code will display all natural numbers in a given range entered by the user.

RESULT :

If user type j = 5 k = 9

and click **Natural No**, the output will be:

5

6

7

8

9

❖ ADDITION USING JAVASCRIPT

JavaScript code for adding two numbers and displaying the result on the webpage.

```
<script>

var a=78;

var b=88;
```

```
var c=parseInt(a)+parseInt(b);

document.write(c);

</script>
```

RESULT : 166

EXPLANATION :

✓ Two variables, a and b, are assigned

values 78 and 88.

✓ parseInt() ensures the values are treated

as integers.

✓ The sum is stored in variable c.

✓ document.write(c) outputs the result directly on the webpage.

❖ *ADD USER INPUT USING POST METHOD*

HTML , JavaScript code for adding two numbers entered by the user and displaying the result on the webpage.

<HTML>

<HEAD>

```
<script>

function sum()

{

var

a=document.getElementById("N1").value;

var

b=document.getElementById("N2").value;

var c=parseInt(a)+parseInt(b);

//document.write(c);
```

```
document.getElementById("aa").innerHT

ML=c;

}

</script>

</HEAD>

<BODY>

first number<INPUT TYPE="TEXT"

ID="N1">

second number<INPUT TYPE="TEXT"

ID="N2">
```

```
<button type="button" id="f"

onclick="sum()">add</button>

<p id="aa"></p>

</BODY>

</HTML>
```

RESULT :

If user type first number =3 and second

number= 6 and then click add the page

will show 9

❖ ARRAYS IN JAVASCRIPT

HTML , JavaScript code for **accessing a specific element from an array and displaying it on the webpage**.

```
<html>

<head>

</head>

<body>

<p id="s"></p>
```

```
<script>

var a=['n','m','o','p','q'];

document.getElementById("s").innerHT

ML=a[3];

</script>




</body>

</html>
```

EXPLANATION :

a is an array containing:

Index 0 - 'n'

Index 1 - 'm'

Index 2 - 'o'

Index 3 - 'p'

Index 4 - 'q'

a[3] retrieves the 4th item - "p".

document.getElementById("s").innerHT

ML puts that value inside the <p>

element with id="s".

RESULT : p

❖ *USING HTML & JAVASCRIPT TO DISPLAY A SELECTED BACKGROUND IMAGE*

HTML + JavaScript code for selecting a file from your computer, extracting its name, and displaying it in an <img> tag.

```html
<html>

<head>

<script>

function previewImage(event) {

var file = event.target.files[0];

if (file) {

var imageURL =

URL.createObjectURL(file);
```

```
      document.getElementById("u").src =

      imageURL;

    }

  }

</script>

</head>

<body>

<!-- File input -->

<input type="file" accept="image/*"

onchange="previewImage(event)">
```

```html
<!-- Image preview -->

<img src="" id="u" style="max-width:300px; margin-top:10px;">

</body>

</html>
```

COLOR ON CHANGE

❖ USING JAVASCRIPT PROGRAM UPDATE A <P> ELEMENT (ID="P") BASED ON USER INPUTS:

HTML + JavaScript code for **live text editing and styling** — letting the user type text, change its color, background, and width interactively.

```
<!DOCTYPE html>
<html>
```

```
<head>

<script>

function updateText(a) {

document.getElementById("p").innerHT

ML = a;

}



function changeTextColor(b) {

document.getElementById("p").style.colo

r = b;
```

```
}

function changeBackgroundColor(h) {

document.getElementById("p").style.bac

kgroundColor = h;

}

function changeWidth(j) {

document.getElementById("p").style.widt

h = j + "px";

}
```

```html
</script>

</head>

<body><textarea

onkeyup="updateText(this.value)"

placeholder="Type here..."></textarea>

<br><br>


<label>Text Color:</label>
```

```
<input type="color"

onchange="changeTextColor(this.value)"

>

<br><br>


<label>Background Color:</label>

<input type="color"

onchange="changeBackgroundColor(this.

value)">

<br><br>
```

```html
<label>Width (in pixels):</label>

<input type="number"

onchange="changeWidth(this.value)"

min="50" max="500" step="10">

<br><br>

<p id="p" style="border: 1px solid black;

padding: 10px; display: inline-

block;">Your text will appear here</p>

</body>

</html>
```

RESULT:

User type - the paragraph updates instantly.

User pick colors - text and background change.

User enter a width - the box resizes.

❖ *CREATE A REGISTRATION FORM USING PHP*

<html>

```
<head>

<script>

function aa(p)

{

var n=/^[a-z A-Z]+$/;

if(p.match(n))

{

document.getElementById("a").innerHT
ML="";

}
```

```javascript
else

{

document.getElementById("a").innerHT

ML="INVALID DATA";

}


}

function bb(q)

{
```

```
var b=/^[0-9]+$/;

if(q.match(b))

{

document.getElementById("b").innerHT
ML="";


}

else

{
```

```javascript
document.getElementById("b").innerHT

ML="INVALID DATA";

}

}

function cc(r)

{

var c=r.length;

if (c>8 && c<=12)

{
```

```
document.getElementById("d").innerHT

ML="";

}

else

{

document.getElementById("d").innerHT

ML="PASSWORD SHOULD BE

BETWEEN 8-12";

}

}
```

```javascript
function ww()

{

var

f=document.getElementById("n1").check

ed;

var

g=document.getElementById("n2").check

ed;

if(f==false && g==false)

{
```

```javascript
alert("Select your gender");

return false;

}

var

h=document.getElementById("m1").chec

ked;

var

i=document.getElementById("m2").check

ed;
```

```javascript
var
j=document.getElementById("m3").checked;
if(h==false && i==false && j==false)
{


    alert("select language");


    return false;
}
```

```html
}

</script>

</head>

<body>

<form method="POST">

<table style="color: pink;background-color: hotpink;font-family:  cursive;width:55% ;height:44%"
>
```

```html
<tr><td>NAME </td><td><input

type="text"

onkeyup="aa(this.value)"><span id="a">

</span></td></tr>

<tr><td>AGE</td><td><input

type="text" onkeyup="bb(this.value)"

><span id="b"></span></td></tr>

<tr><td>ADDRESS </td><td><textarea

id="c"></textarea></td></tr>

<tr><td>PASSWORD</td><td><input

type="password"
```

```html
onkeyup="cc(this.value)"><span

id="d"></span></td></tr>

<tr><td>GENDER</td><td><input

type="radio" id="n1"

value="male"/>male

<input type="radio" id="n2"

value="female"/>female</td></tr>


<tr><td>LANGUAGE</td><td><input

type="checkbox" id="m1"

value="english"/>english
```

```html
<input type="checkbox"  id="m2"
value="hindi"/>hindi
<input type="checkbox"
id="m3"  value="french"/>french</td></t
r>


<tr><td>STATE</td><td>
<select><option>
New york
</option>
```

```html
<option>

Los angels

</option>

<option>

Toronto

</option>

</select></td></tr>

<tr><td><input type="submit"

value="submit" onclick="return

ww()"></td></tr>
```

</form>

</body>

</html>

EXPLANATION:

➢ Name validation (aa() function)

➢ Uses the regex /^[a-z A-Z]+$/ [Allows only letters and spaces. Shows "INVALID DATA" if the name contains numbers or special characters.]

➢ Age validation (bb() function). Uses /^[0-9]+$/   Allows only digits. Shows

"INVALID DATA" if letters or special characters are entered.

➤ Password validation (cc() function). Checks password length between 8 and 12 characters. Displays error message if not in range.

➤ Gender selection check (ww() function)- Makes sure either "male" or "female" is selected. Shows alert if both are unchecked.

➤ Language selection check- Ensures at least one language checkbox is ticked. Alerts if none are selected.

➤ Other form fields - State: Dropdown with "New york", "Los angels", "Toronto".

➤ Submit button runs ww() to verify required selections.

❖ *FORM VALIDATION*

ENSURES THE DATA ENTERED BY USERS IS CORRECT, IT GIVES IMMEDIATE FEEDBACK TO USERS.

```
<html>

<head>

<script>
```

```
function yy(s)

{

var r=/^[a-z A-Z]+$/;

if(s.match(r))

{

document.getElementById("n11").style.b
order="none";

document.getElementById("p").innerHT
ML="";

}
```

```
else

{

document.getElementById("n11").style.b
order="red 2px solid";

document.getElementById("p").innerHT
ML="INVALID DATA";

}

}

function GG(m)

{
```

```javascript
var d=/^[0-9]+$/;

if(m.match(d))

{

document.getElementById("n22").style.border="none";

document.getElementById("b").innerHTML="";

}

else

{
```

```
document.getElementById("n22").style.b

order="red 2px solid";

document.getElementById("b").innerHT

ML="INVALID DATA";

}

}

function MM(o)

{

var f=/^[0-9]+$/;

if(o.match(f))
```

```
{
document.getElementById("n33").style.border="none";

document.getElementById("z").innerHTML="";

}

else

{

document.getElementById("n33").style.border="red 2px solid";
```

```javascript
document.getElementById("z").innerHT

ML="INVALID DATA";

}

}

function QQ(x)

{

var nt=x.length

if(nt>=8 && nt<13)

{
```

```
document.getElementById("n44").style.b
order="none";

document.getElementById("v").innerHT
ML="STRONG PASSWORD";

}

else

{

document.getElementById("n44").style.b
order="red 2px solid";
```

```javascript
document.getElementById("v").innerHTML="PASSWORD SHOULD BE BETWEEN 8-12";



}

}

function zz()

{
```

```javascript
var
t=document.getElementById("d").checke
d;
var
y=document.getElementById("e").checke
d;
if(t==false && y==false)
{
alert("choose your gender");
return false;
```

```javascript
}

var
n=document.getElementById("c1").check
ed;

var
m=document.getElementById("c2").chec
ked;

var
o=document.getElementById("c3").check
ed;
```

```
var
p=document.getElementById("c4").check
ed;

if(n==false && m==false && o==false
&& p==false)

{

alert("choose your language");

return false;

}

}
```

```html
</script>

</head>

<body>

<form method="POST">

<div class="container">

<div class="col-auto">


<table class="table table-responsive table-
bordered" style="background-color:
```

black;font-family: inherit;color:

#fefefe">

<tr><td>NAME:</td><td><input

type="text" id="n11"

onkeyup="yy(this.value)" ><span

id="p"></span>
</td></tr>

<tr><td>AGE:</td><td><input

type="text" onkeyup="GG(this.value)"

id="n22"><span

id="b"></span>
</td></tr>

```html
<tr><td>PHONE NO:</td><td><input
type="text" onkeyup="MM(this.value)"
id="n33"><span
id="z"></span><BR/></td></tr>

<tr><td>PASSWORD:</td><td><input
type="password"
onkeyup="QQ(this.value)"
id="n44"><span
id="v"></span></td></tr>

<tr><td>ADDRESS:</td><td><textarea
id="c"></textarea><BR/></td></tr>
```

```html
<tr><td>GENDER:</td><td><input
type="radio" id="d" name="g"
value="male"/>male

<input type="radio" id="e" name="g"
value="female"/>female<BR/></td></tr>


<tr><td>LANGUAGE:</td><td><input
type="checkbox" name="f"
id="c1"/>ENGLISH
```

```html
<input type="checkbox" name="f"
id="c2" />MALAYALAM

<input type="checkbox" name="f"
id="c3"/>HINDI

<input type="checkbox" name="f"
id="c4"/>FRENCH<BR/></td></tr>


<tr><td>STATE:<select id="i">

<option>California</option>

<option>Los angels</option>
```

```html
<option>New york</option>

</select><BR/></td></tr>


<tr><td><input type="SUBMIT"
value="ok"  onclick="return
zz()"></td></tr>

</TABLE>

</div></div>

</FORM>

</body>
```

</html>

EXPLANATION :

➢ Name (yy() function)

➢ Only letters and spaces allowed (/^[a-z A-Z]+$/). Invalid entries get a red border + "INVALID DATA" message.Valid entries remove the border and clear the error.

- Age (GG() function) - Only digits allowed. Invalid entries get a red border + "INVALID DATA" message.

- Phone Number (MM() function). Only digits allowed

- Password (QQ() function). Must be between 8 and 11 characters. If valid - border removed + "STRONG PASSWORD" message.If invalid - red border + "PASSWORD SHOULD BE BETWEEN 8-12".

- Gender Selection (zz() function). Must pick male or female. Alerts if neither selected.

- Language Selection. At least one checkbox must be ticked. Alerts if none selected.

- Other Fields. Address: Textarea

- State: Dropdown with "California", "Los angels", and "New york".

❖ *CREATE A REGISTRATION FORM WITH CLIENT-SIDE VALIDATION USING JAVASCRIPT AND BOOTSTRAP FOR STYLING.*

The form includes:

- **Name validation (only alphabets)**
- **Age & Phone Number validation (only digits)**
- **Password strength check (8-12 characters)**
- **Gender selection validation**

- **Language selection validation**

- **Dropdown for State selection**

- **Submit & Reset buttons**

```html
<html>

<head>

<link href="bootstrap-3.3.7-dist/css/bootstrap.min.css" rel="stylesheet" type="text/css"/>

<script>

function validateName(s) {
```

```javascript
var r = /^[a-zA-Z\s]+$/;

var inputField =
document.getElementById("n11");

var errorMsg =
document.getElementById("p");


if (r.test(s)) {

inputField.style.border = "2px solid
green";

errorMsg.innerHTML = "";
```

```javascript
  } else {

    inputField.style.border = "2px solid red";

    errorMsg.innerHTML = "Invalid Name
    (Only letters allowed)";

  }

}


function validateAge(m) {

  var d = /^[0-9]{1,2}$/;
```

```javascript
var inputField =

document.getElementById("n22");

var errorMsg =

document.getElementById("b");



if (d.test(m)) {

inputField.style.border = "2px solid

green";

errorMsg.innerHTML = "";

} else {
```

```javascript
inputField.style.border = "2px solid red";

errorMsg.innerHTML = "Invalid Age
(Only numbers allowed)";

}

}

function validatePhone(o) {

var f = /^[0-9]{10}$/;

var inputField =
document.getElementById("n33");
```

```javascript
var errorMsg =
document.getElementById("z");


if (f.test(o)) {

inputField.style.border = "2px solid
green";

errorMsg.innerHTML = "";

} else {

inputField.style.border = "2px solid red";
```

```
errorMsg.innerHTML = "Invalid Phone

(Must be 10 digits)";


}


}



function validatePassword(x) {

var inputField =

document.getElementById("n44");

var errorMsg =

document.getElementById("v");
```

```
if (x.length >= 8 && x.length <= 12) {

inputField.style.border = "2px solid

green";

errorMsg.innerHTML = "<span

style='color:green;'>Strong

Password</span>";

} else {

inputField.style.border = "2px solid red";
```

```
errorMsg.innerHTML = "<span

style='color:red;'>Password should be 8-

12 characters</span>";

}

}


function validateForm() {

var genderChecked =

document.querySelector('input[name="g"]

:checked');
```

```
var languageChecked =

document.querySelectorAll('input[name=

"f"]:checked');



if (!genderChecked) {

alert("Please choose your gender.");

return false;

}



if (languageChecked.length === 0) {
```

```
    alert("Please select at least one

    language.");

    return false;

    }

    return true;

    }

</script>

</head>


<body>
```

```html
<form method="POST" onsubmit="return validateForm();">

<div class="container">

<div class="col-auto">

<table class="table table-responsive table-borderless text-center" style="width: 100%; background-color: #2aabd2; color: #761c19;">

<center>
```

```html
<h2 style="background-color: #2aabd2;
color: #761c19;">REGISTRATION
FORM</h2>

</center>

<tr>

<td>NAME:</td>

<td><input type="text" id="n11"
onkeyup="validateName(this.value)"><sp
an id="p"></span></td>

</tr>
```

```html
<tr>

<td>AGE:</td>

<td><input type="text"

onkeyup="validateAge(this.value)"

id="n22"><span id="b"></span></td>

</tr>

<tr>

<td>PHONE NO:</td>
```

```html
<td><input type="text"
onkeyup="validatePhone(this.value)"
id="n33"><span id="z"></span></td>
</tr>
<tr>
<td>PASSWORD:</td>
<td><input type="password"
onkeyup="validatePassword(this.value)"
id="n44"><span id="v"></span></td>
</tr>
```

```html
<tr>

<td>ADDRESS:</td>

<td><textarea id="c"></textarea></td>

</tr>

<tr>

<td>GENDER:</td>

<td>

<input type="radio" id="d" name="g"

value="male"/>Male
```

```html
<input type="radio" id="e" name="g"
value="female"/>Female

</td>

</tr>

<tr>

<td>LANGUAGE:</td>

<td>

<input type="checkbox" name="f"
id="c1"/>ENGLISH
```

```html
<input type="checkbox" name="f"
id="c2"/>MALAYALAM

<input type="checkbox" name="f"
id="c3"/>HINDI

<input type="checkbox" name="f"
id="c4"/>FRENCH

</td>

</tr>

<tr>

<td>STATE:</td>
```

```html
<td>

<select id="i">

<option>California</option>

<option>Los angels</option>

<option>New york</option>

</select>

</td>

</tr>

<tr>

<td></td>
```

```html
<td>

<input type="submit"

value="REGISTER" class="btn btn-

primary">

<button type="reset" class="btn btn-

secondary">RESET</button>

</td>

</tr>

</table>

</div>
```

```
</div>

</form>

</body>

</html>
```

❖ FIND GRADE USING JAVASCRIPT

```
<html>

<head>

<SCRIPT>

function yy(a)
```

```
{

if(a>90 && a<100)

{

document.getElementById("p").innerHT

ML="GRADE A";

}

else if( a>100)

{
```

```javascript
document.getElementById("p").innerHT

ML="invalid data";

}

else if(a>80)

{

document.getElementById("p").innerHT

ML="GRADE B";

}

else if(a>70)

{
```

```javascript
document.getElementById("p").innerHT

ML="GRADE C";

}

else

{

document.getElementById("p").innerHT

ML="GRADE D";

}

}

</SCRIPT>
```

```
</head>

<body>

<input type="text"

onkeyup="yy(this.value)">

<p id="p"></p>

</body>

</html>

Java1

<html>

<head>
```

```
<script>

function CHK1()

{

document.getElementById("U").innerHT

ML="PHP: Hypertext Preprocessor) is a

widely-used open source general-purpose

scripting language that is especially suited

for web development and can be

embedded into HTML.";

}

function CHK2()
```

```javascript
{

document.getElementById("V").innerHT

ML="Hypertext Markup Language

(HTML) is the standard markup language .

It can be assisted by technologies such as

Cascading Style Sheets (CSS) and

scripting languages such as JavaScript";

}

function CHK3()

{
```

```
document.getElementById("W").innerHT

ML="CSS stands for Cascading Style

Sheets. CSS describes how HTML

elements are to be displayed on screen,

paper, or in other media.";

}

</script>

</head>

<body>

<button id="U" onclick="CHK1()">

php</button>
```

```html
<button id="V"
onclick="CHK2()">html</button>

<button id="W"
onclick="CHK3()">css</button>

</body>

</html>
```

EXPLANATION :

When a user fills in their details (name, age, phone, etc.), the JavaScript functions check whether the input is valid **as they type** (live validation).

If something is wrong, the form shows an error message or highlights the field in red.

➢ Name - Only letters and spaces allowed

➢ Age - Only numbers allowed, 1–2 digits

➢ Phone Number - Must be exactly 10 digits

➢ Password - Must be between 8–12 characters

- Gender - User must choose Male or Female

- Language - User must choose at least one

- Uses Bootstrap for styling (buttons, table layout, colors).

- Changes border color (green/red) to show valid/invalid inputs.

- When the user types in a field - onkeyup calls a validation function. The function checks the value against a regex or length rule. If valid - border turns green, error message clears. If invalid - border turns red, error message shows.

➢ On clicking REGISTER - validateForm() runs - if any required option (gender/language) is missing - alert shows - form doesn't submit.

It helps prevent wrong data from being sent to the server.

❖ USING JAVA SCRIPT FIND WHETHER THE NUMBER GIVEN IS ODD OR EVEN

```
<HTML>

<head>

<script>

function AA(a)

{

if(a%2==1)
```

```
{

document.getElementById("P").innerHT

ML="odd";

}

else

{

document.getElementById("P").innerHT

ML="even";

}

}
```

```
</script>

<BODY>

<INPUT TYPE="TEXT"
onkeyup="AA(this.value)">

<p id="P"></p>

</BODY>

</HTML>
```

EXPLANATION:

➢ User input - You type a number in the <input> box. onkeyup runs the AA() function every time you release a key.

➢ Function logic (AA(a)): Checks if a % 2 == 1 - number is odd. Else - number is even.

➢ Result - Shows "odd" or "even" inside the <p> element with id="P".

RESULT :

Example

Type 5 - Output: odd

Type 4 - Output: even

❖ *FIND IF SOMEONE IS*

MARRIAGABLE AGE OR NOT

[FEMALE 18 YEARS OLD, MALE

21 YEARS OLD]

<html>

```
<head>

<script>

function sub()

{

var

a=document.getElementById("s").value;

var

b=document.getElementById("m").check

ed;
```

```javascript
var
c=document.getElementById("f").checke
d;


if(a>=18 && c==true )

{

document.getElementById("p").innerHT
ML="AGE TO MARRY";

}

else if(a>=21 && b==true )
```

```
{

document.getElementById("p").innerHT

ML="AGE TO MARRY";

}

else

{

document.getElementById("p").innerHT

ML="NOT AGE TO MARRY";

}

}
```

```html
</script>

</head>

<body>

AGE<input type="text" id="s"><br/>

GENDER<input type="radio" id="m"
name="g"/>male

<input type="radio" id="f"
name="g"/>female<br/>

<input type="button" value="check"
onclick="sub()">
```

```
<p id="p"></p>

</body>

</html>
```

RESULT:

If User type Age and Gender - selected via radio buttons (male or female).

Condition checks in sub() function:

If age $\geq$ 18 and gender is female - show "AGE TO MARRY".

Else if age ≥ 21 and gender is male -

show "AGE TO MARRY".

Otherwise - "NOT AGE TO MARRY".

ONBLUR

<html>

<head>

<script>

function AA()

{

```
var
a=document.getElementById("A").value;
document.getElementById("s").innerHT
ML=a;
}
</script>
</head>
<body>
ENTER NAME<input type="text"
id="A" onblur="AA()">
```

```
<p id="s"></p>

</body>

</html>
```

EXPLANATION :

User type name in the <input> box. The onblur="AA()" event runs when you move the cursor away from the input (click elsewhere or press Tab).

Function AA(): Gets the value you typed.

❖ *CHANGE TEXT ON CLICK*

A Javascript , HTML code in which clicking the heading changes its text:

```
<html>

<head>

<script>

function CHK()

{
```

```
document.getElementById("R").innerHT
ML="trinity technologies";
}
</SCRIPT>
</head>
<body>
<H1 ID="R"
onclick="CHK()">TRINITY</H1>
</body>
</html>
```

EXPLANATION:

At first, the page shows the heading **TRINITY**.

The onclick="CHK()" in the <h1> tag means that when you click the heading, the CHK() function will run.

Function CHK() Finds the <h1> element with id="R".

Replaces its content from "TRINITY" to "trinity technologies".

❖ *HIDE A TEXT BOX*

Given below is a JavaScript code written using jQuery.

If user open this below given code in a browser with jQuery loaded, clicking the text box will instantly make it disappear.

<html>

<head>

<!-- Load jQuery from CDN -->

```
<script
src="https://code.jquery.com/jquery.min.j
s" type="text/javascript"></script>
<script>
$(document).ready(function() {
  $("input").click(function() {
    $("input").hide();
  });
});
</script>
<title></title>
</head>
```

```
<body>

<input type="text">

</body>

</html>
```

When an <input> is clicked, it hides all input fields on the page.

JQUERY

jQuery is a JavaScript library. It makes working with JavaScript easier, it can do animations and effects, it handles mouse movements and clicks.

For example :

Without jquery javascript code would be long like this:

```
document.getElementById("btn").addEve
ntListener("click", function() {
```

```
document.getElementById("message").te
xtContent = "Hi!";
```

```
});
```

With jquery same javascript code would be :

```
$("#btn").click(function() {
```

```
$("#message").text("Hi!");

});
```

❖ **jQuery example that hides a paragraph when it's clicked.**

You load a webpage, it will show the text Hello, click on it, and it vanishes.

```
<html>
```

```html
<head>

<script src="jquery-3.4.1.min.js"
type="text/javascript"></script>

<script>

$(document).ready(function()

{

$("p").click(function()

{

$("p").hide();

});
```

```
});

</script>

<meta charset="UTF-8">

<title></title>

</head>

<body>

<p>Hello</p>

</body>

</html>
```

❖ *FIND HEIGHT OF AN IMAGE*

Javacsript jquery code to find height of an image:

```html
<html>

<head>

<!-- Load jQuery from CDN -->

<script

src="https://code.jquery.com/jquery-

3.4.1.min.js"></script>
```

```
<script>

$(document).ready(function(){

  $("#btn").click(function(){

    var height = $("#r").height();

    $("#s").text(height + "px");

  });

});

</script>

</head>

<body>
```

```html
<img src="folder/1.jpg" alt="Sample Image" id="r" height="55px"/>

<br/>

<button type="button" id="btn">HEIGHT</button>

<p id="s"></p>

</body>

</html>
```

EXPLANATION:

Uses $("#r").height() — jQuery's method for getting element height.

Uses $("#s").text() instead of innerHTML.

Added $(document).ready() so the code runs only after the page is loaded.

RESULT :

Loads jQuery from a local file (jquery-3.4.1.min.js)

Displays an image (folder/1.jpg) with a height of 55px.

When you click the HEIGHT button, the qq() function runs:

It gets the .height property of the image with ID r.

Then it puts that number into the <p> element with ID s.

❖ HIDE OR SHOW A PARAGRAPH

```
<html>

<head>

<!-- Load jQuery from official CDN -->

<script

src="https://code.jquery.com/jquery-

3.4.1.min.js"></script>

<script>

$(document).ready(function(){

    $("#hideBtn").click(function(){

        $("p").hide();
```

```
        });

    $("#showBtn").click(function(){

        $("p").show();

    });

});

</script>

</head>

<body>

<p>I AM LEARNING

PROGRAMMING</p>

<button type="button"

id="showBtn">Show</button>
```

```html
<button type="button"
id="hideBtn">Hide</button>
</body>
</html>
```

EXPLANATION:

$("#hideBtn") - Selects the button with id="hideBtn".

.click(function(){ ... }) - Runs the inside code when that button is clicked.

$("p").hide() - Selects all <p> elements and hides them.

RESULT :

User open the page.

jQuery loads.

When user click Hide, all <p> text disappears.

When user click Show, the text comes back.

❖ FOCUS OR BLURR

- *USES JQUERY TO CHANGE THE BACKGROUND COLOR OF INPUT FIELDS WHEN THEY GAIN OR LOSE FOCUS.*

```html
<html>

<head>
```

```
<script src="jquery-3.4.1.min.js"
type="text/javascript"></script>


<script>
$(document).ready(function()
{
$("input").focus(function()
{
$(this).css("background-color", "orange");
});
```

```
$("input").blur(function()

{

$(this).css("background-color", "pink");

});

});

</script>

</head>

<body>

<input type="text" name="f"><br>

<input type="text" name="e">
```

```
</body>
```

```
</html>
```

· *WHEN A USER CLICKS INSIDE ANY INPUT FIELD, IT TURNS orange.*

· *WHEN THE USER CLICKS OUTSIDE (OR MOVES TO ANOTHER FIELD), IT TURNS pink.*

● *FADE IN OR FADE OUT*

```
<!DOCTYPE html>
```

```
<html>
```

```html
<head>

<meta charset="UTF-8">

<title>Fade In and Fade Out

Example</title>


<!-- jQuery Library -->

<script src="jquery.min.js"></script>



<style>

.dd {
```

background-color: orange;

width: 200px;

height: 100px;

margin: 20px;

padding: 5%;

position: relative;

text-align: center;

line-height: 100px;

font-size: 18px;

font-weight: bold;

```
color: white;

}

</style>

<script>

$(document).ready(function () {

$("#b1").click(function () {

$("#a1").fadeOut(700);

$("#a2").fadeIn(2000);

});

$("#b2").click(function () {
```

```
$("#a1").fadeIn(2000);

$("#a2").fadeOut(2000);

});

 $("#a2").click(function () {

$(this).animate({ left: '100px', top: '100px',

fontSize: '2em' }, 2000)

.animate({ left: '-100px', top: '-100px' },

2000);

});

});
```

```html
</script>

</head>

<body>

<button id="b1">Fade Out / Fade In</button><button id="b2">Fade In / Fade Out</button>

<div class="dd" id="a1">Box 1</div>

<div class="dd" id="a2" style="display:none;">Box 2</div>

</body>
```

</html>

RESULT:

Click "Fade Out / Fade In" - Box 1 fades out, Box 2 fades in.

Click "Fade In / Fade Out" - Box 1 fades in, Box 2 fades out.

Click Box 2 - It moves diagonally, increases font size, then moves back.

❖ PRESS BUTTON INORDER TO HIDE THE GIVEN PARAGRAPH.

```html
<html>

<head>

<script src="jquery-3.4.1.min.js"
type="text/javascript"></script>

<script>

$(document).ready(function()

{

$("button").click(function()
```

```
        {

        alert("jnj");

        $("p").hide();

    });

    });

    </script>

    <title></title>

    </head>

    <body>

    <button type="button">ok</button>
```

```html
<p>huhjijkkkjkk</p>

</body>

</html>
```

● *HIDE OR SHOW*

```html
<html>

<head>

<script src="jquery-3.4.1.min.js"

type="text/javascript"></script>

<script>

$(document).ready(function()
```

```
{

$("#s1").click(function()

{

$("#q").show();

$("#r").hide();

});

$("#s").click(function()

{

$("#r").show();

$("#q").hide();
```

```html
});

});

</script>

</head>

<body>


<img src="folder/1.jpg" alt="" id="r"/>

<img src="folder/2.jpg" alt="" id="q"/>

<br/>
```

```html
<button type="button"
id="s">ON</button>

<button type="button"
id="s1">OFF</button>

</body>

</html>
```

❖ *ANIMATION*

USING HTML, CSS, and jQuery code animate two div elements (#a and #b) when the button with ID #q is clicked.

```
<!DOCTYPE html>

<html>

<head>

<style>

.ss {
```

```css
    width: 100px;

    height: 100px;

    background-color: red;

    position: absolute;

    top: 300px;

    left: 300px;

}

.ll {

    width: 100px;

    height: 100px;
```

```
background-color: pink;

position: absolute;

top: 50px;

left: 50px;

}

</style>

<!-- jQuery CDN -->

<script

src="https://code.jquery.com/jquery-

3.6.0.min.js"></script>
```

```
<script>

$(document).ready(function() {

$("#q").click(function() {

$("#a").animate({ top: '700px', left:

'0px' }, 2000)

.animate({ top: '0px', left: '30px' }, 2000)

.animate({ top: '700px', left: '0px' }, 2000)

.animate({ top: '0px', left: '90px' }, 2000)
```

```
.animate({ top: '300px', left: '200px' },

2000);

$("#b").animate({ top: '700px', left:

'1000px' }, 2000)

.animate({ top: '700px', left: '700px' },

2000);

});

 $("#w").click(function() {

$("#a, #b").fadeOut(2000);

});
```

```
$("#fadeIn").click(function() {

$("#a, #b").fadeIn(2000);

});

});

</script>

</head>

<body>

<button id="q">Start Animation</button>

<button id="w">Fade Out</button>

<button id="fadeIn">Fade In</button>
```

```html
<div class="ss" id="a"></div>

<div class="ll" id="b"></div>

</body>

</html>
```

❖ ANIMATE

```html
<HTML>

<HEAD>

<style>

.dd
```

```
{

background-color: orange;

width: 200px;

height: 100px;

padding: 5%;

z-index: 1;

position: absolute;

}

.mm

{
```

```css
background-color: pink;

width: 200px;

height: 100px;

padding: 5%;

position: absolute;

top: 50px;

left: 50px;

}

</style>
```

```html
<script src="jquery-
3.4.1.min.js" type="text/javascript"></scr
ipt>

<script>

$(document).ready(function()

{

$("#a2").click(function()

{

$("#a2").animate({left:
'50px',top:'50px',fontSize:'2em'},2000);
```

```
$("#a1").animate({left:
'0px',top:'0px',fontSize:'2em'},2000);

$("#a2").css("z-index","-1");

});

});

</script>

<body>

<div class="dd" id="a2"> athi lourdes
mount</DIV>
```

```html
<div class="mm" id="a1">lourdes

mount</DIV>

</BODY>

</HTML>
```

AJAX

❖ AJAX (Asynchronous JavaScript and XML)

It enables communication between the client (browser) and the server to fetch data **asynchronously.** It is a technique used in web development, it's not a programming language.

Uses : Search suggestions that appear as you type.

Filtering & Sorting Data Example: Amanzon website update products lists instantly when you choose sort by (Best sellers, Above 4 star review)

AJAX will make web pages feel faster and more interactive because it allows web pages to update dynamically without reloading. Eg: Updation of stock market prices.

Example :

```php
<?php

mysql_connect("localhost","root","");

mysql_select_db("school");

?>

<html>

<head>

<script>

function dis(a)

{

var xmlhttp=new XMLHttpRequest();
```

```
xmlhttp.onreadystatechange=function()

{

if(this.readyState==4 &&

this.status==200)

{

document.getElementById("p").innerHT

ML=this.responseText;

}

}
```

```
xmlhttp.open("GET","COUNTRY.php?q
="+a,true);

xmlhttp.send();

}

</script>

</head>

<body>

<?php

$SEL=mysql_query("select * from
country");
```

```php
?>

<select onchange="dis(this.value)">

<option>choose</option>

<?PHP

while($f=mysql_fetch_row($SEL))

{

?>

<option value="<?Php ECHO

$f[0] ?>"><?Php ECHO

$f[1] ?></option>
```

```php
<?PHP

}

?>

</select>

<?php

echo mysql_error();

?>

<div id="p"></div>

</body>

</html>
```

● LOAD COUNTRY

```php
<?php

mysql_connect("localhost","root","");

mysql_select_db("school");

IF(ISSET($_POST['S']))

{

$A=$_POST['A'];

mysql_query("insert into country values

('','$A')");

}
```

```
?>

<html>

<HEAD>

</HEAD>

<BODY>

<form method="POST">

ADD COUNTRY <INPUT

TYPE="TEXT" NAME="A">

<INPUT TYPE="SUBMIT" NAME="S"

VALUE="SUBMIT">
```

</FORM>

</BODY>

</html>

- **LOAD DISTRICT**

```php
<?php

mysql_connect("localhost","root","");

mysql_select_db("school");

IF(ISSET($_POST['S']))

{

$A=$_POST['A'];
```

```php
mysql_query("insert into country values

(",'$A')");

}

?>
```

```html
<html>

<HEAD>

</HEAD>

<BODY>

<form method="POST">
```

ADD COUNTRY <INPUT

TYPE="TEXT" NAME="A">

<INPUT TYPE="SUBMIT" NAME="S"

VALUE="SUBMIT">

</FORM>

</BODY>

</html>

- **LOAD STATE**

<?php

mysql_connect("localhost","root","");

```php
mysql_select_db("school");

$ID=$_GET['q'];

echo $ID;

$SEL=mysql_query("select * from state
where country='$ID'");

?>

<select  NAME="M">

<option>choose</option>

<?PHP

while($f=mysql_fetch_row($SEL))
```

```php
{
?>

<option value="<?Php ECHO

$f[0] ?>"><?Php ECHO

$f[1] ?></option>

<?PHP

}

?>

</select>
```

BOOTSTRAP

Bootstrap is a **front-end framework** that helps you quickly design and build **responsive, mobile-friendly websites.**

Responsive layout - Your website adjusts automatically to different screen sizes (mobile, tablet, desktop).

Ready-made components - Buttons, forms, navigation bars, modals, etc.

Consistent styling - Built-in colors, typography, and spacing rules.

Example :

```
<!DOCTYPE html>
<html lang="en">
<head>
<meta charset="UTF-8">
<meta name="viewport" content="width=device-width, initial-scale=1">
```

```html
<title>Short Bootstrap Example</title>
<link
href="https://cdn.jsdelivr.net/npm/bootstr
ap@5.3.3/dist/css/bootstrap.min.css"
rel="stylesheet">
</head>
<body class="p-4">


<h1 class="text-primary">Hello!</h1>
<button class="btn btn-success">Click
Me</button>
```

```html
</body>

</html>

<!DOCTYPE html>
```

EXPLANATION :

● <html lang="en">

Declares html and sets language to english.

● <head>

<meta charset="UTF-8">

\<meta name="viewport"

content="width=device-width, initial-

scale=1">

charset="UTF-8" - allows all standard

characters.

viewport - makes the website responsive

on mobile screens.

- \<link

href="https://cdn.jsdelivr.net/npm/boot

strap@5.3.3/dist/css/bootstrap.min.css"

rel="stylesheet">

Links to **Bootstrap's CSS** via **CDN**

- **<body class="p-4">**

Starts the page body.

p-4 is a Bootstrap spacing class

- **<h1 class="text-primary">Hello!</h1>**

<h1> - heading.

text-primary - applies Bootstrap's

"primary" (pink) text color.

- **<button class="btn btn-success">Click Me</button>**

<button> - creates a clickable button.

btn - makes it look like a styled Bootstrap button.

btn-success - applies green color.

- **</body>**

</html>

body and HTML closing tag.

CSS

CSS stands for Cascading Style Sheets —
it's the language used to style HTML
pages (colors, fonts, layouts, sizes,
animations, etc.).

EXAMPLE:

<!DOCTYPE html>

<html>

<head>

```html
<title>CSS Example</title>

<style>

body {

background-color: pink;

}

h1 {

color: red;

font-family: Arial, sans-serif;

}

</style>

</head>

<body>
```

```
<h1>Hello, CSS!</h1>

<p>This text is styled using CSS.</p>


</body>

</html>
```

EXPLANATION:

background-color: pink; - changes page background to pink.

color: red; - makes the heading red.

font-family: Arial - changes the font.

➤ ALL TAGS - HTML

Text / Content

<h1> to <h6> → Headings

<p> → Paragraph

 → Line break

<hr> → Horizontal line

<span> → Inline text

<div> → Block container

Tables

<table>, <tr>, <td>, <th>, <thead>,

<tbody>, <tfoot>

Lists

<dl>, <dt>, <dd>

<ul>, <ol>, <li>

Formatting

<b>, <u>, <i>,<mark>, <strong>, <em>, <small>, <big>,<del>, <ins>, <sup>, <sub>

Links & Media

<a href=""> → Link

<img src=""> → Image

<video>, <audio>, <source>

Semantic

<header>, <footer>, <nav>, <section>, <article>, <aside>, <main>

Forms

<form>, <input>, <select>,

<option>,<textarea>, <button>, <label>,

<fieldset>, <legend>

Others

<script>, <style>, <link>, <meta>, <title>

➤ **ALL CSS → PROPERTIES**

 Text/Font: color, font-size, font-family,

line-height,text-align,

Background: background-color, background-image, background-size

Positioning: position, top, left,float, z-index

Effects: box-shadow, animation,opacity, transition.

Box Model: margin, padding, border, width, height

Flex/Grid: display:flex;, grid-template-columns

➤ BOOTSTRAP → CLASSES

Layout

container, container-fluid, row, col-

Components

btn, btn-primary, btn-danger,navbar,

navbar-brand, navbar-nav

card, card-body, card-header

alert, badge, , accordion, dropdown,

breadcrumb modal, carousel

Text & Colors

text-center, text-primary, text-muted, bg-dark, bg-light

Utilities

Spacing: m-1, p-3, mt-2, mb-4

Display: d-block, d-none, d-flex

Flex: justify-content-center, align-items-start

➢ PHP/JS → CODE & FUNCTIONS

PHP has functions, variables, loops, conditions.

Echo/Print: echo, print

Functions: function myFunc(){}

Conditions: if, else, switch

Loops: for, foreach, while, do while

Arrays: array(), []

Superglobals: $_POST, $_GET, $_SESSION, $_COOKIE

➢ JAVASCRIPT

JS has functions, events, DOM methods,

Variables: var, let, const

Conditions: if, else, switch

Functions: function(){}, arrow ()=>{}

Loops: for, while, forEach

DOM

document.getElementById(),
querySelector()

innerHTML, style, classList

Events

onclick, onchange, onmouseover,
onsubmit

> **AJAX/JQUERY → METHODS**

jQuery selectors + functions.

Selectors

$("#id"), $(".class"), $("p")

Effects

.hide(), .show(), .fadeIn(), .fadeOut(), .slid
eUp(), .slideDown()

DOM

.html(), .text(), .val(), .attr(), .css()

Events

.click(), .hover(), .change(), .submit()

➢ AJAX

$.get(), $.post(), $.ajax()

www.ingramcontent.com/pod-product-compliance
Lightning Source LLC
LaVergne TN
LVHW051221050326
832903LV00028B/2193